WAR MOVIE POSTERS

volume thirteen of
the illustrated history of movies through posters

Images from the Hershenson-Allen Archive

Previous Volumes:
Volume One: Cartoon Movie Posters
Volume Two: Cowboy Movie Posters
Volume Three: Academy Award Winners' Movie Posters
Volume Four: Sports Movie Posters
Volume Five: Crime Movie Posters
Volume Six: More Cowboy Movie Posters
Volume Seven: Horror Movie Posters
Volume Eight: Best Pictures' Movie Posters
Volume Nine: Musical Movie Posters
Volume Ten: Serial Movie Posters
Volume Eleven: Horror, Sci-Fi & Fantasy Movie Posters
Volume Twelve: Comedy Movie Posters

Edited by Richard Allen and Bruce Hershenson
Published by Bruce Hershenson
P.O. Box 874, West Plains, MO 65775
Phone: (417) 256-9616 Fax: (417) 257-6948
mail@brucehershenson.com (e-mail)
http://www.brucehershenson.com or
http://www.emovieposter.com (website)

IF YOU ENJOYED THIS MOVIE POSTER BOOK,
THEN YOU ARE SURE TO ENJOY THESE
OTHER SIMILAR BRUCE HERSHENSON
PUBLICATIONS. LOOK FOR THEM AT YOUR
LOCAL BOOKSTORE OR ORDER
THEM DIRECT FROM THE PUBLISHER.
ORDER YOUR COPY OF
ATTACK OF THE B MOVIE POSTERS TODAY!

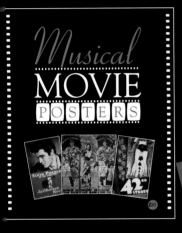

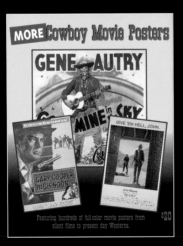

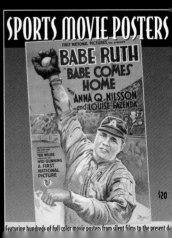

INTRODUCTION

Welcome to the thirteenth volume of the Illustrated History of Movies Through Posters. The subject of this book, war movies, has been one of the most popular genres since the beginning of film, as the drama, action, violence, and life-and-death situations inherent in a war film are always popular at the box office. But there have been far too many war films made to cover in a single volume, so I had to establish some guidelines in what would be included.

I could have limited the book solely to films that are primarily concerned with actual battles, but I felt this was too limiting. Therefore, I have also included films concerning related matters, such as espionage, prisoners of war, the home front, returning home, etc. But expanding my scope just made it that much more difficult to choose which films to include, as it meant I needed to pick a few hundred images from out of over 2000!

Far more films have been made about World War II than any other war, so roughly half of this volume is devoted to that war, and I have presented those posters according to the segment of the war they cover. I made every effort to correctly determine the primary subject matter of each World War II film, but it is probable that some errors were made, and I ask that anyone seeing an error of fact let me know, so I can correct it in a future edition.

I also chose to include a section of posters that concern the period known as The Cold War. While not a "war" in the conventional sense, there was always the potential for the destruction of the entire planet, and so I felt those films deserved being included in this volume!

Finally, since this is a book of images, I tried to always give preference to posters that have the most visual appeal, although I have also tried to include images from all the best known war films. If a personal favorite of yours is missing, it is possible that I was unable to locate a poster from that film.

This book would never have been published without my partner, Richard Allen. War films are a favorite genre of Richard's and he has spent many years tracking down elusive titles. The organization of this book was Richard's idea and he was the source of most of the images. Just about everything about this volume is due to Richard's involvement (except for any errors that have crept in, which are solely mine!).

Unless otherwise noted, each image in this volume is of the original U.S. one-sheet poster (the standard movie poster size, measuring 27" x 41"), from the first release of the film. Other sizes included are lobby cards (11" x 14"), window cards (14" x 22"), inserts (14" x 36"), half-sheets (22" x 28"), three-sheets (41" x 81"), six-sheets (81" x 81"), and foreign posters (varying sizes).

All the images in this book come from the Hershenson-Allen Archive. The archive consists of over 35,000 different movie poster images, all photographed directly from the original posters onto high quality 4" x 5" color transparencies. There is not another resource like it anywhere, and it is the world's foremost source of movie poster images. The Archive has provided images for books, videos, DVDs, magazines, and newspapers.

This is not a catalog of posters for sale, nor do I sell any sort of movie poster reproductions! However, I do sell movie posters of all sorts through public auctions, both "live" and over the Internet. If you are interested in acquiring original vintage movie posters (or any of the other books I have published) visit my website at http://www.brucehershenson.com (the most visited vintage movie poster site on the Internet) or send me a self-addressed stamped envelope for free brochures.

There are a few dealers who went out of their way to locate posters for this volume. Kirby McDaniel (Movie Art in Austin, Texas) was the source of the six-sheet to Memphis Belle and the one-sheet for Pershing's Crusaders. Kirby has been in the movie poster hobby for decades, and he has a particular love of six-sheets. Other dealers who were very helpful were Mike Orlando (Hollywood Canteen), Larry Toth (J. Fields Gallery), and John Hazelton. Thanks very much!

I need to thank Amy Knight who did the layouts and designed the covers for this book, and Sylvia Hershenson, who assisted in its preparation and did the proofreading. Most of all, I need to thank my partner, Richard Allen. He has always loved movie posters of all years and genres, and he tracked down many of the images in this book. We share a common vision, and we hope to keep publishing these volumes until we have covered every possible genre of film.

I dedicate this book to my daughter, Hayley Suzanne Hershenson. Although she is only little over a year old, she has already become a major presence in the Hershenson household, and Sylvia, Holden, Luke and myself cannot imagine how we managed without her!

Bruce Hershenson
November 2000

GLOSSARY

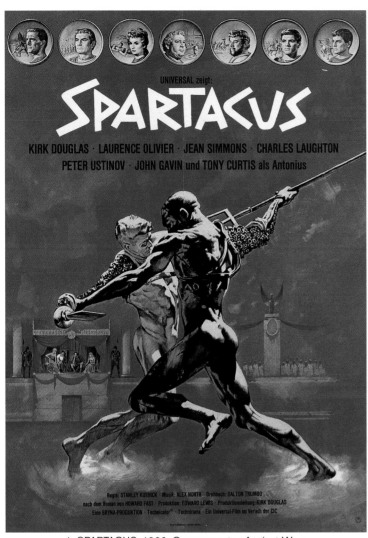

1. SPARTACUS, 1960, German poster, Ancient Wars

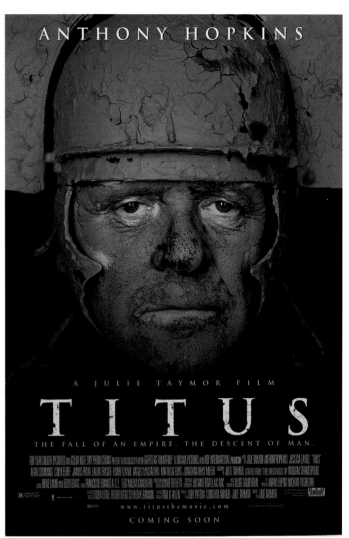

2. TITUS, 1999, Ancient Wars

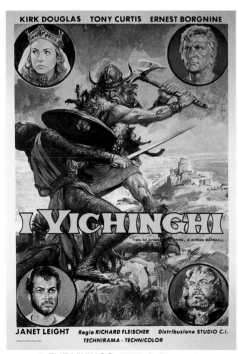

3. THE VIKINGS, 1958, Italian poster,
Medieval Wars

4. EL CID,1961, 1980s reissue, Spanish Wars

5. ALEXANDER NEVSKY, 1939, Italian poster,
Russian Wars

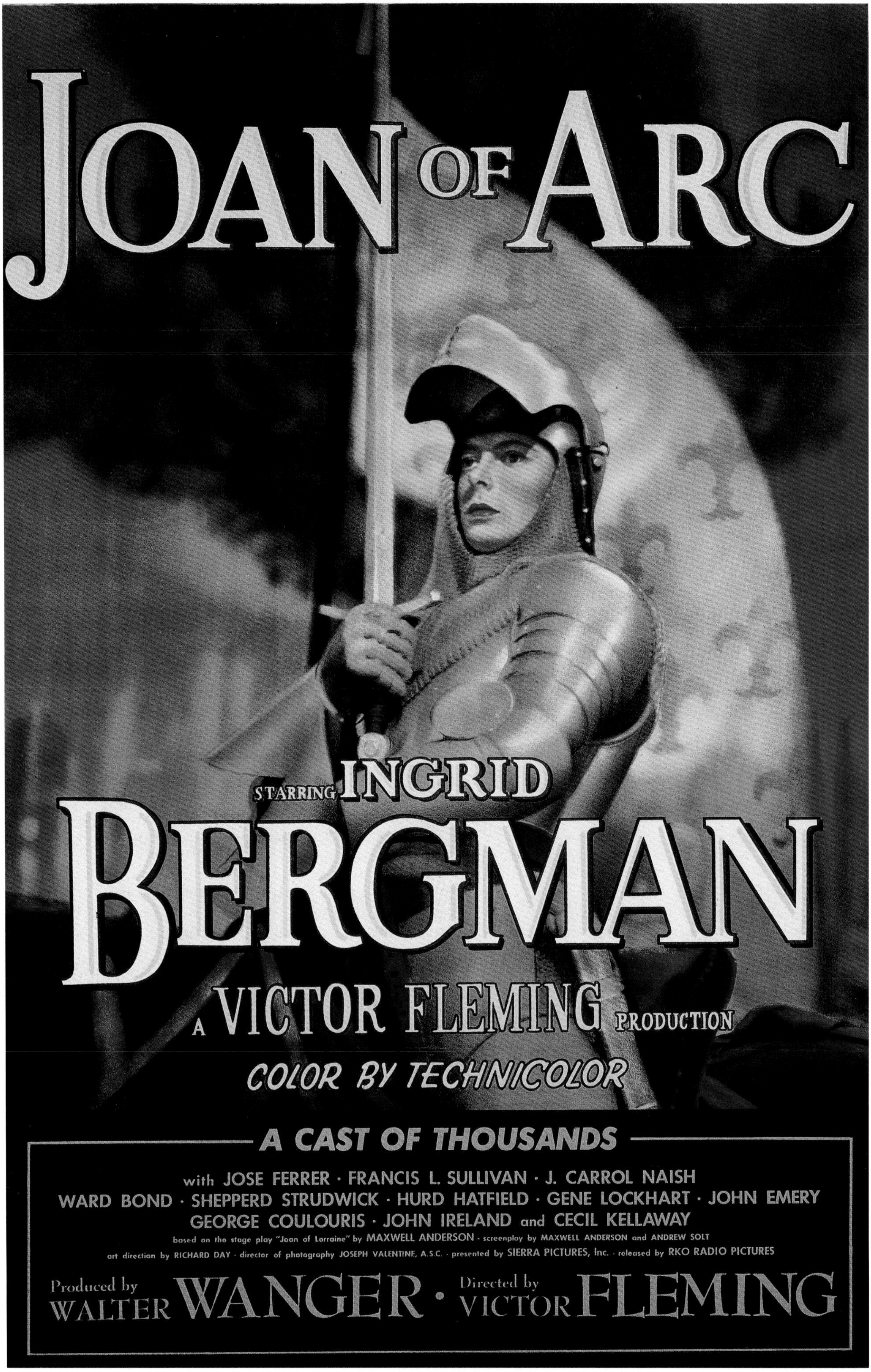

6. JOAN OF ARC, 1948, French Wars, Medieval Times

7. THE MESSENGER (JEANNE D'ARC), 1999, French poster,
French Wars, Medieval Times

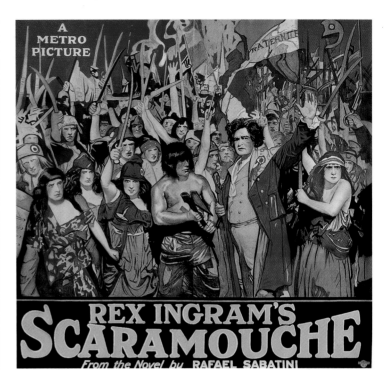

8. SCARAMOUCHE, 1923, six-sheet, French Revolution

9. NAPOLEON (NAPOLEON BONAPARTE), 1927, French Wars, Napoleonic

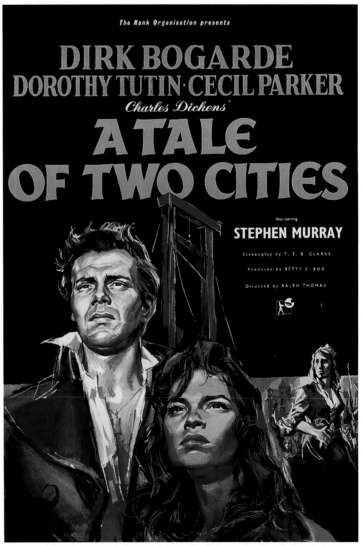

10. A TALE OF TWO CITIES, 1956, English poster, French Revolution

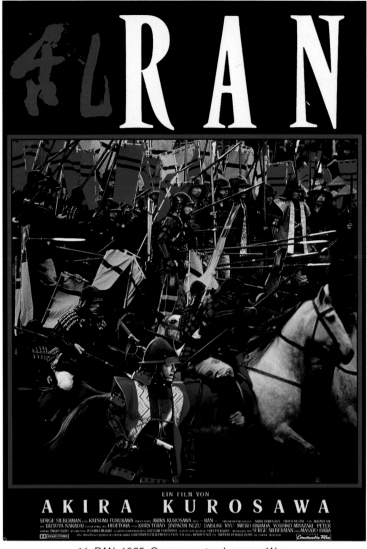

11. RAN, 1985, German poster, Japanese Wars

12. THE SEVEN SAMURAI, 1956 (1990s reissue), Japanese Wars

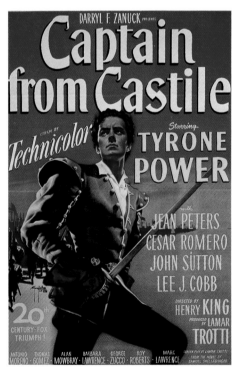

13. CAPTAIN FROM CASTILE, 1947,
Spanish Wars

14. THE PRIDE AND THE PASSION, 1957, British quad, Spanish Wars

15. WAR AND PEACE, 1956, Russian Wars

16. THE BATTLESHIP POTEMKIN, 1925, Russian poster, Russian Revolution

17. 1917 A.D., year unknown, Russian poster, Russian Revolution

18. THE SAND PEBBLES, 1966, Italian poster, China Wars

19. FOR WHOM THE BELL TOLLS, 1943, Spanish Civil War

20. EXCALIBUR, 1981, British Wars, Medieval Times

21. PRINCE VALIANT, 1954, six-sheet, British Wars, Medieval Times

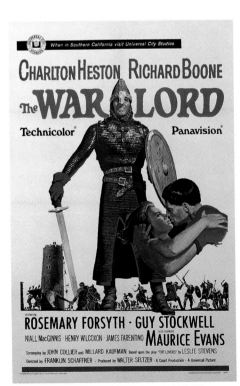

22. THE WAR LORD, 1965, British Wars,
Medieval Times

23. THE CRUSADES, 1935, British Wars,
Third Crusade

24. BRAVEHEART, 1995, British Wars,
Scottish Rebellion

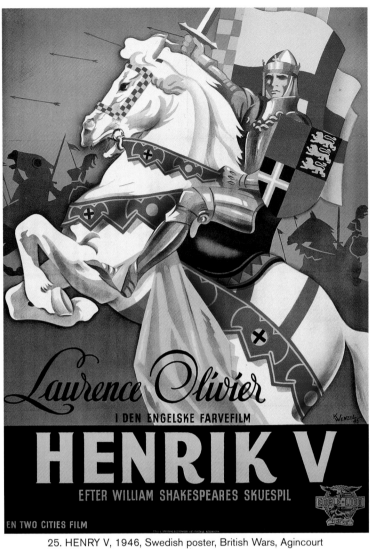

25. HENRY V, 1946, Swedish poster, British Wars, Agincourt

26. FIRE OVER ENGLAND, 1937, British Wars, Spanish Armada

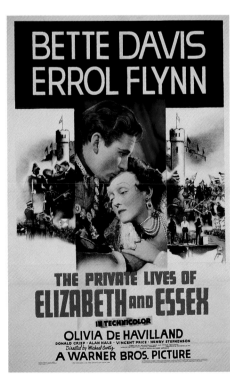

27. THE PRIVATE LIVES OF ELIZABETH AND ESSEX, 1939, British Wars, Elizabethan Era

28. CROMWELL, 1970, British Wars, Civil War

29. ROB ROY, 1995, British Wars, Scottish Revolt

30. CAPTAIN HORATIO HORNBLOWER, 1951, Italian poster,
British Wars, Naval

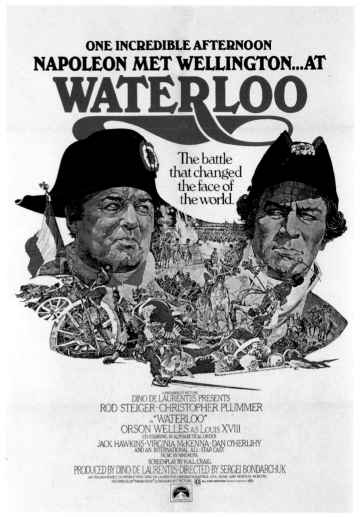

31. WATERLOO, 1970, British Wars, Napoleonic

32. THE CHARGE OF THE LIGHT BRIGADE, 1936,
French poster, British Wars, Crimea

33. BREAKER MORANT, 1980,
Australian daybill, British Wars, Boer

34. MICHAEL COLLINS, 1996, British Wars,
Irish Rebellion

35. BEAU GESTE, 1939, British Wars, Africa

36. THE LIVES OF A BENGAL LANCER, 1935, British Wars, India

37. WEE WILLIE WINKIE, 1937, British Wars, India

38. GUNGA DIN, 1939, Italian poster,
British Wars, India

39. ZULU, 1964, British Wars, Africa

40. THE FOUR FEATHERS, 1929,
British Wars, Africa

41. THE LAST OF THE MOHICANS, 1992, French and Indian War

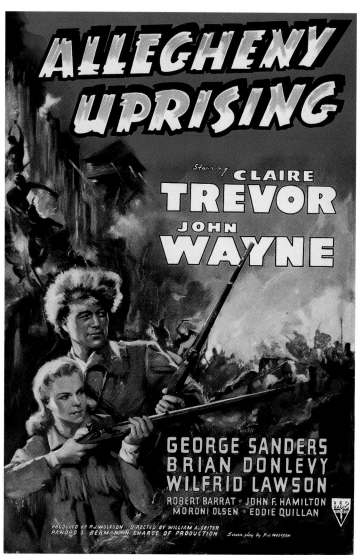

42. ALLEGHENY UPRISING, 1939, Pre-Revolutionary War

43. WASHINGTON CROSSES THE DELAWARE,
1912, French poster, Revolutionary War

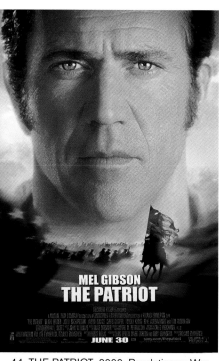

44. THE PATRIOT, 2000, Revolutionary War

45. REVOLUTION, 1985, Revolutionary War

THE
MIDNIGHT RIDE
of
PAUL REVERE

D.W.
GRIFFITH
PRESENTS
AMERICA
· A THRILLING STORY
OF LOVE AND ROMANCE ·
BY ROBERT W. CHAMBERS

MADE IN U.S.A.

© 1924 THE H·C·MINER LITHO CO·N·Y.

46. AMERICA, 1924, window card, Revolutionary War

47. LAST COMMAND, 1955,
Texas Independence

48. THE ALAMO, 1960, Texas Independence

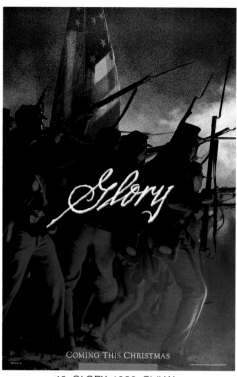

49. GLORY, 1989, Civil War

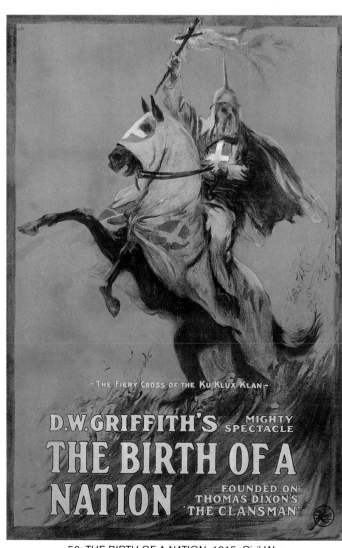

50. THE BIRTH OF A NATION, 1915, Civil War

51. THE LITTLEST REBEL, 1935, special one-sheet, Civil War

52. ABRAHAM LINCOLN, 1924, window card, Civil War

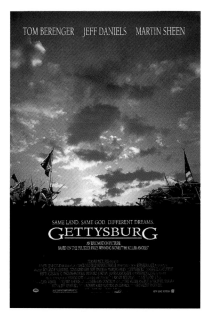

53. GETTYSBURG, 1993, Civil War

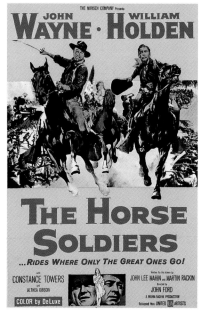

54. THE HORSE SOLDIERS, 1959, Civil War

55. THE GOOD, THE BAD AND THE UGLY, 1967, French poster, Civil War

56. GONE WITH THE WIND, 1939, three-sheet, Civil War

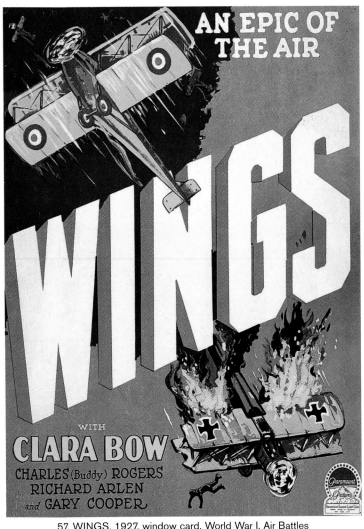

57. WINGS, 1927, window card, World War I, Air Battles

58. HELL'S ANGELS, 1930, Swedish poster, WW I, Air Battles

59. THE DAWN PATROL, 1930, WW I,
Air Battles

60. THE BLUE MAX, 1966, WW I, Air Battles

61. THE RED BARON, 1971, WW I, Air Battles

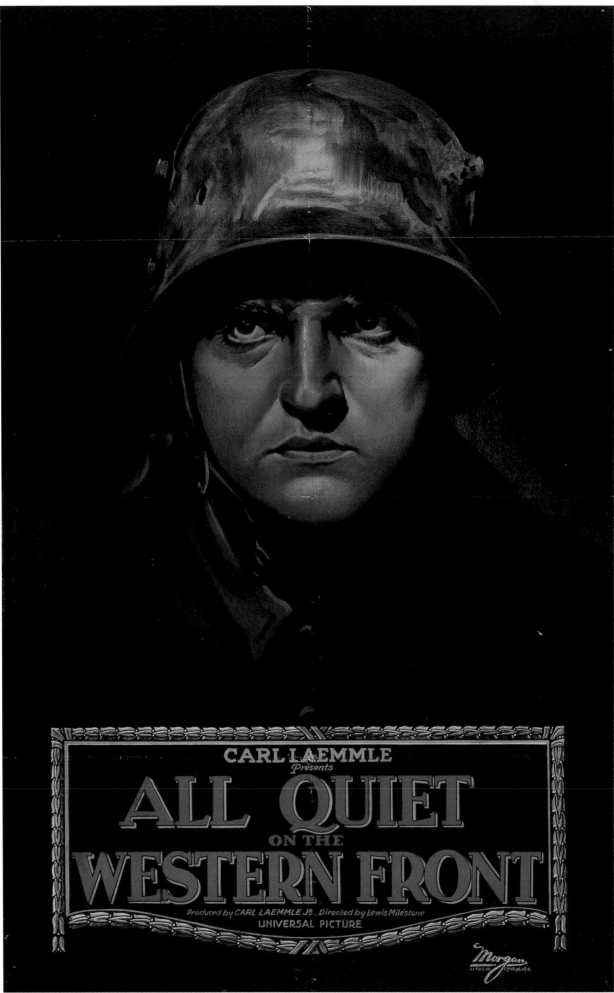

62. ALL QUIET ON THE WESTERN FRONT, 1930, WW I, Western Front

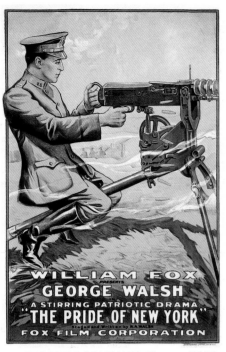

63. THE PRIDE OF NEW YORK, 1917, WW I, Western Front

64. OVER THE TOP, 1918, WW I, Western Front

65. PARAMOUNT BRAY-PICTOGRAPH, c.1918, WW I, Western Front

66. WESTFRONT 1918, 1930, Swedish poster, WW I, Western Front

67. THE GREAT ILLUSION, 1938, Yugoslavian poster, WW I, Western Front

68. ALL QUIET ON THE WESTERN
FRONT, 1930, Italian poster, WW I,
Western Front

69. PATHS OF GLORY, 1957, WW I,
Western Front

70. SERGEANT YORK, 1941, WW I,
Western Front

71. THE BIG PARADE, 1925, three-sheet, WW I, Western Front

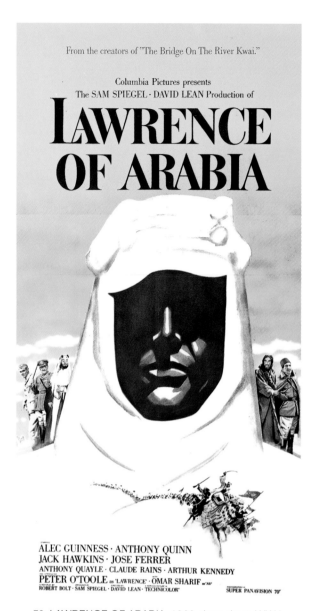

72. LAWRENCE OF ARABIA, 1962, three-sheet, WW I,
Near East

73. A FAREWELL TO ARMS, 1932, WW I, Italy

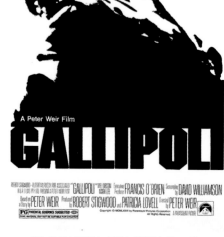

74. THE LOST PATROL, 1934, WW I, Near East

75. GALLIPOLI, 1981, WW I, Near East

76. HEROES ALL, c.1918, WW I, Europe

PERSHING'S CRUSADERS

AUSPICES OF THE

UNITED STATES GOVERNMENT

-THE FIRST OFFICIAL AMERICAN WAR PICTURE-

TAKEN BY U.S. SIGNAL CORPS AND NAVY PHOTOGRAPHERS

77. PERSHING'S CRUSADES, 1918, WW I Documentary

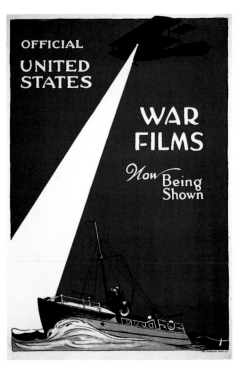

78. OFFICIAL UNITED STATES WAR FILMS
NOW BEING SHOWN, c.1916,
WW I Documentary

79. OUR AMERICAN BOYS IN THE
EUROPEAN WAR, 1916, WW I Documentary

80. IF YOUR SOLDIER'S HIT, c.1917,
WW I Documentary

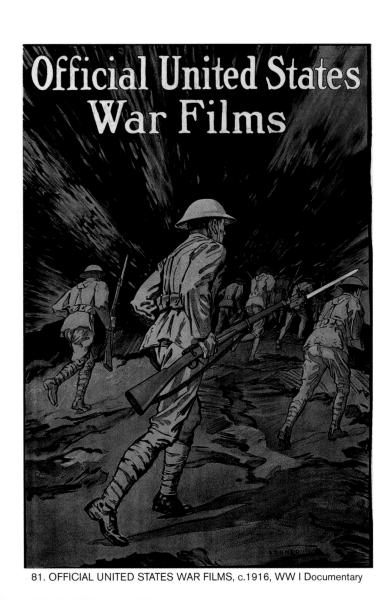

81. OFFICIAL UNITED STATES WAR FILMS, c.1916, WW I Documentary

82. LA CROIX DE GUERRE DES FEMMES, c.1917, WW I Documentary

83. DEVIL DOGS OF THE AIR, 1935, window card, Between the Great Wars

84. THE LOST SQUADRON, 1932, Between the Great Wars

85. MARINES ARE HERE, 1938,
Between the Great Wars

86. WHY THIS WAR, c.1934, three-sheet,
Pro-Preparedness for World War II

87. FORGOTTEN MEN, c.1934,
Pro-Preparedness for WW II

88. THE FIGHT FOR PEACE, 1938,
Pro-Preparedness for WW II

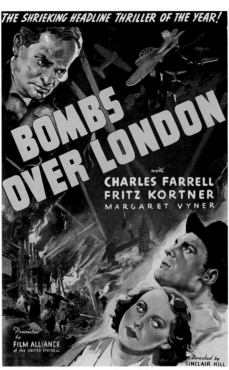

89. BOMBS OVER LONDON (MIDNIGHT
MENACE), 1937, Prelude to WW II

90. CLOUDS OVER EUROPE, 1934,
Prelude to WW II

91. THE COURT-MARTIAL OF BILLY MITCHELL, 1955, Italian poster,
Pro-Preparedness for WW II

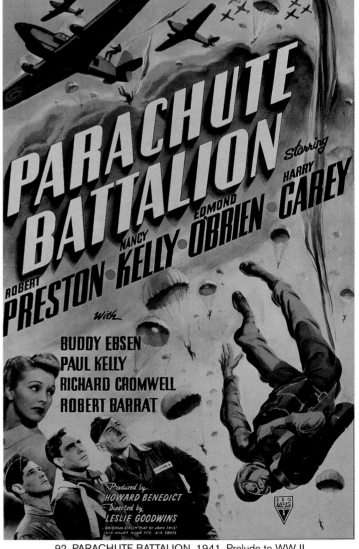

92. PARACHUTE BATTALION, 1941, Prelude to WW II

93. THUNDER BIRDS, 1942,
Prelude to WW II

94. 20,000 MEN A YEAR, 1939,
Prelude to WW II

95. THE GREAT DICTATOR, 1940,
Italian poster, Prelude to WW II

96. I WANTED WINGS, 1941, three-sheet, Prelude to WW II

97. BATTLE OF BRITAIN, 1969, six-sheet, WW II, R.A.F. Air Battles

98. SPITFIRE, 1943, WW II, R.A.F. Air Battles

99. INTERNATIONAL SQUADRON, 1941,
Italian poster, WW II, R.A.F. Air Battles

100. REACH FOR THE SKY, 1956, WW II,
R.A.F. Air Battles

101. A YANK IN THE R.A.F., 1941, WW II,
R.A.F. Air Battles

102. IN WHICH WE SERVE, 1942, Title card, WW II, British Navy

103. SINK THE BISMARCK!, 1960, British quad, WW II, British Navy

104. THE BATTLE OF THE RIVER PLATE, 1956, three-sheet, WW II, British Navy

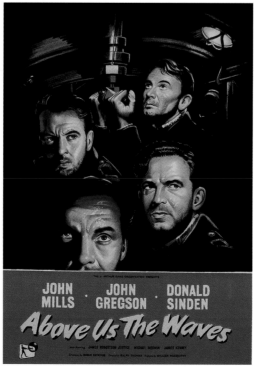

105. ABOVE US THE WAVES, 1956, WW II, British Navy

106. THE VALIANT, 1962, WW II, British Navy

107. THIS ABOVE ALL, 1942, WW II, British Home Front

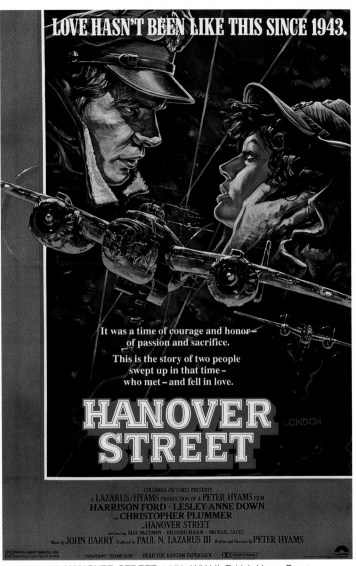

108. HANOVER STREET, 1979, WW II, British Home Front

109. MRS. MINIVER, 1942, WW II,
British Home Front

110. A GUY NAMED JOE, 1943, WW II,
British Home Front

111. HOPE AND GLORY, 1987, WW II,
British Home Front

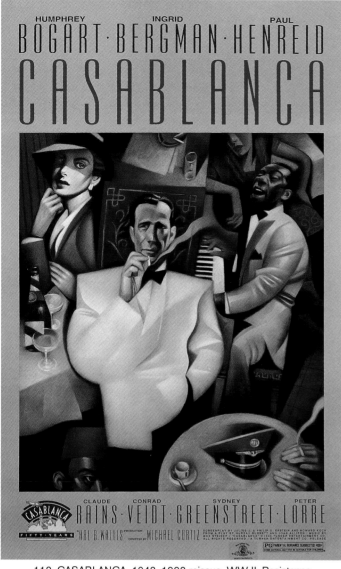

112. CASABLANCA, 1942, 1992 reissue, WW II, Resistance

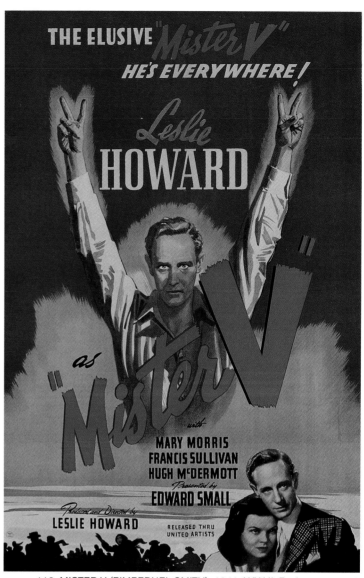

113. MISTER V (PIMPERNEL SMITH), 1941, WW II, Resistance

114. SECRET AGENT OF JAPAN, 1942, WW II,
Japan the Enemy

115. FIRST YANK INTO TOKYO, 1945, WW II,
Japan the Enemy

116. BLOOD ON THE SUN, 1945, WW II,
Japan the Enemy

117. THE HOUR BEFORE THE DAWN, 1944, WW II, Espionage

118. THEY CAME TO BLOW UP AMERICA, 1943, WW II, Espionage

119. CODE NAME EMERALD, 1985, WW II, Espionage

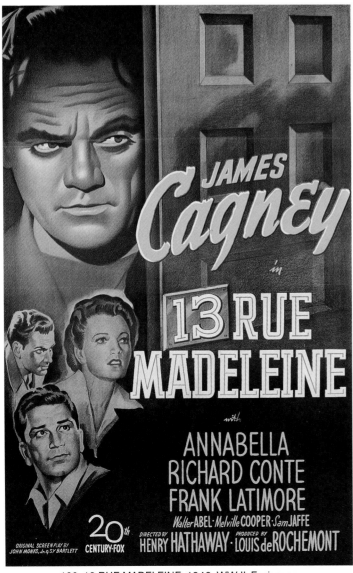

120. 13 RUE MADELEINE, 1946, WW II, Espionage

121. MADAME SPY, 1942, WW II, Espionage

122. ACTION IN THE NORTH ATLANTIC, 1943, Title card, WW II, North Atlantic

123. CRASH DIVE, 1943, WW II, North Atlantic

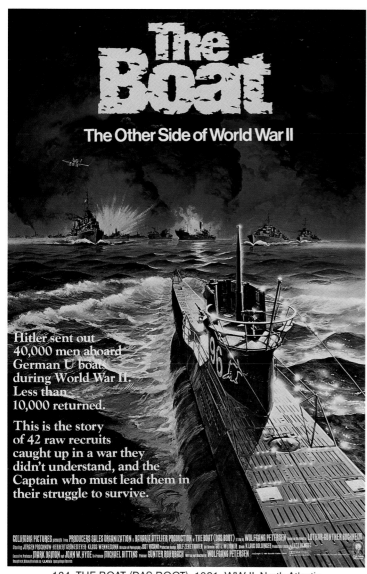

124. THE BOAT (DAS BOOT), 1981, WW II, North Atlantic

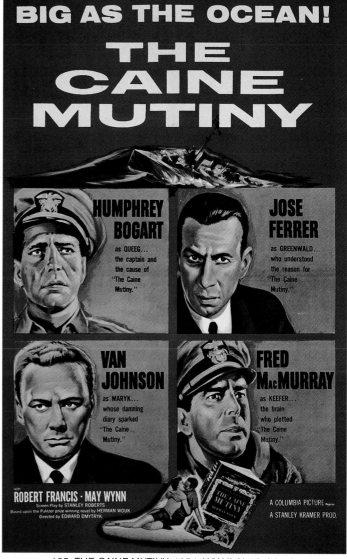

125. THE CAINE MUTINY, 1954, WW II, North Atlantic

126. FIVE GRAVES TO CAIRO, 1943, WW II,
North Africa

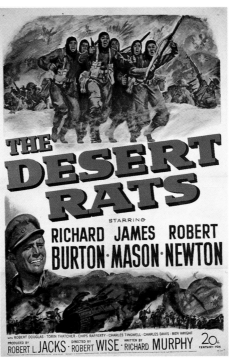

127. THE DESERT RATS, 1953, WW II,
North Africa

128. THE ENGLISH PATIENT, 1996, WW II,
North Africa

129. SAHARA, 1943, WW II, North Africa

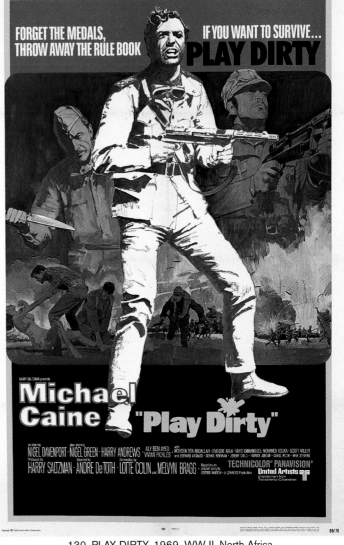

130. PLAY DIRTY, 1969, WW II, North Africa

132. THE STORY OF G.I. JOE, 1945, Title card, WW II,
European Land Battles

133. THE LONGEST DAY, 1962, British quad, WW II D-Day

131. A WALK IN THE SUN, 1945, WW II, three-sheet,
European Land Battles

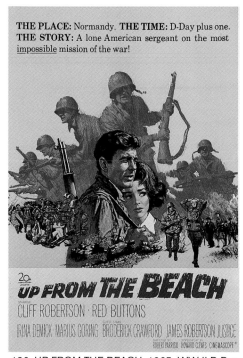

134. A BRIDGE TOO FAR, 1977, WW II,
European Land Battles

135. SAVING PRIVATE RYAN, 1998,
WW II D-Day

136. UP FROM THE BEACH, 1965, WW II D-Day

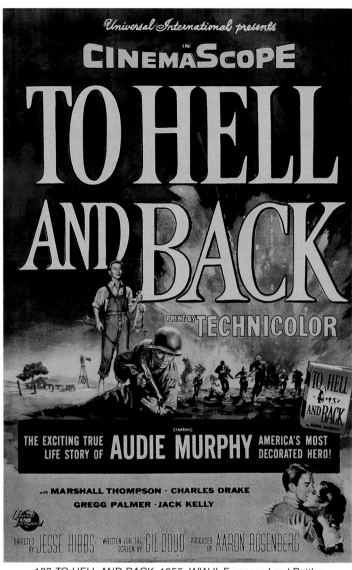

137. TO HELL AND BACK, 1955, WW II, European Land Battles

138. PATTON, 1969, Italian poster, WW II, European Land Battles

139. HELL IS FOR HEROES, 1962, WW II,
European Land Battles

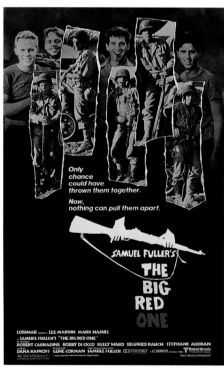

140. THE BIG RED ONE, 1980, WW II,
European Land Battles

141. BATTLE OF THE BULGE, 1965, WW II,
European Land Battles

142. BATTLEGROUND, 1949, WW II,
European Land Battles

143. THE TRAIN, 1965, WW II,
European Land Battles

144. CASTLE KEEP, 1969, WW II,
European Land Battles

145. GO FOR BROKE!, 1951, WW II, European Land Battles

146. CROSS OF IRON, 1977, WW II, European Land Battles

147. COMMANDOS STRIKE AT DAWN, 1942, WW II, Suicide Missions

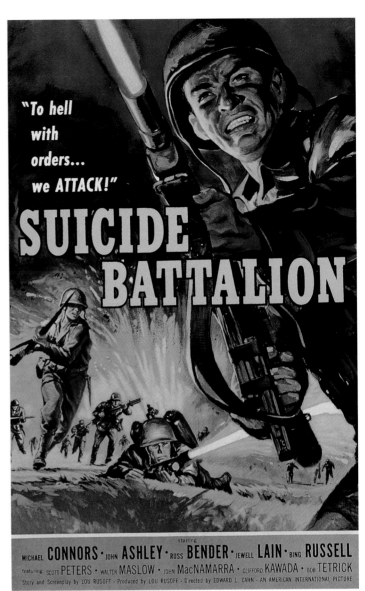

148. SUICIDE BATTALION, 1958, WW II, Suicide Missions

149. THE EAGLE HAS LANDED, 1976, WW II, Suicide Missions

150. TONIGHT WE RAID CALAIS, 1943, WW II, Suicide Missions

151. THE YOUNG LIONS, 1958, WW II, Suicide Missions

152. THE DIRTY DOZEN, 1957, German poster, WW II, Suicide Missions

153. STALAG 17, 1953, 1959 reissue, WW II, European P.O.W.s

154. THE PASSWORD IS COURAGE, 1962, WW II, European P.O.W.s

155. VON RYAN'S EXPRESS, 1965, WW II, European P.O.W.s

156. VICTORY, 1981, WW II, European P.O.W.s

157. SLAUGHTERHOUSE-FIVE, 1972, WW II, European P.O.W.s

158. THE GREAT ESCAPE, 1963, French poster, WW II, European P.O.W.s

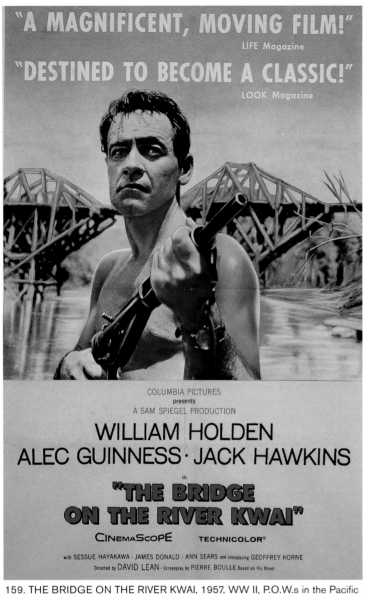

159. THE BRIDGE ON THE RIVER KWAI, 1957, WW II, P.O.W.s in the Pacific

160. A TOWN LIKE ALICE, 1958, English poster, WW II, P.O.W.s in the Pacific

161. EMPIRE OF THE SUN, 1987, WW II, P.O.W.s in the Pacific

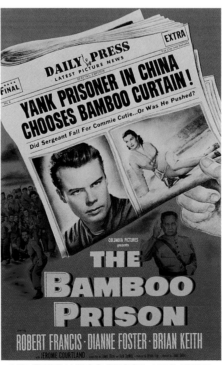

162. THE BAMBOO PRISON, 1955, WW II, P.O.W.s in the Pacific

163. MERRY CHRISTMAS, MR. LAWRENCE, 1982, WW II, P.O.W.s in the Pacific

164. THE MEMPHIS BELLE, 1944, six-sheet, WW II, European Air Battles

165. TWELVE O'CLOCK HIGH, 1949, WW II, European Air Battles

166. ONE OF OUR AIRCRAFT IS MISSING!, 1941, WW II, European Air Battles

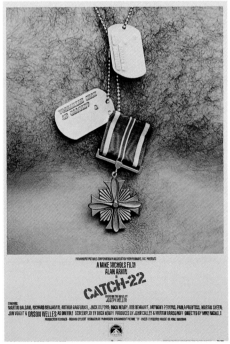

167. CATCH-22, 1970, WW II, European Air Battles

168. THE WAR LOVER, 1962, Italian poster, WW II, European Air Battles

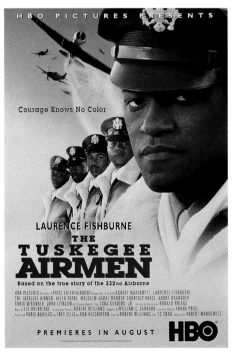

169. THE TUSKEGEE AIRMEN, 1995, WW II, European Air Battles

170. BEHIND THE SCENES IN NAZI
GERMANY, c.1939, WW II, Documentary

171. PRELUDE TO WAR, 1943, WW II,
Documentary

172. BLITZ ON BRITAIN, 1960, WW II,
Documentary

173. TARGET FOR TONIGHT, 1941, WW II, Documentary

174. UNITED WE STAND, 1942, WW II, Documentary

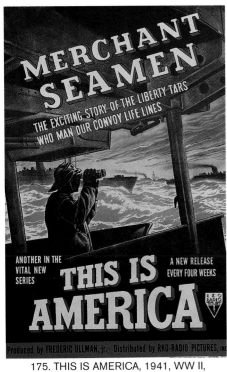

175. THIS IS AMERICA, 1941, WW II,
Documentary

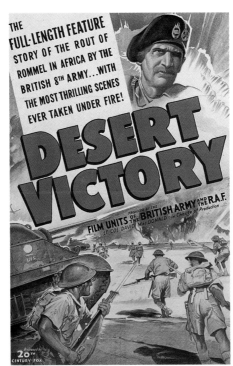

176. DESERT VICTORY, 1943, WW II,
Documentary

177. WE ARE THE MARINES, 1942, WW II,
Documentary

178. THE MEMPHIS BELLE, 1943, WW II, Documentary

179. TUNISIAN VICTORY, 1944, WW II, Documentary

180. TRIUMPH OF THE WILL, 1934,
German poster, WW II, Hitler's Europe

181. HITLER'S CHILDREN, 1942, three-sheet,
WW II, Hitler's Europe

182. HITLER'S MADMAN, 1943, three-sheet,
WW II, Hitler's Europe

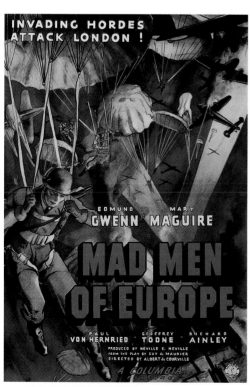

183. MAD MEN OF EUROPE, 1940, WW II,
Hitler's Europe

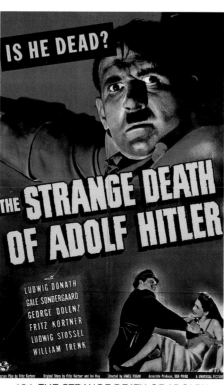

184. THE STRANGE DEATH OF ADOLPH
HITLER, 1943, WW II, Hitler's Europe

185. NAZI LOVE CAMP, 1977, WW II,
Hitler's Europe

186. NONE SHALL ESCAPE, 1944,
three-sheet, WW II, Hitler's Europe

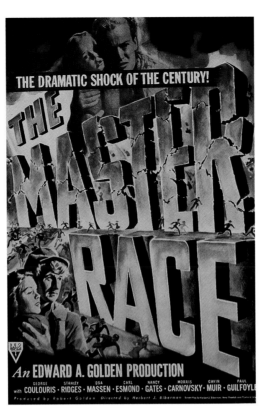

187. THE MASTER RACE, 1944, WW II,
Hitler's Europe

188. THE DIARY OF ANNE FRANK, 1959, WW II,
Hitler's Europe

189. SCHINDLER'S LIST, 1993, WW II, Hitler's Europe

190. LIFE IS BEAUTIFUL, 1997, WW II, Hitler's Europe

191. FROM HERE TO ETERNITY, 1953,
WW II, Pearl Harbor

192. TORA! TORA! TORA!, 1970, WW II,
Pearl Harbor

193. EAGLE OF THE PACIFIC, 1953,
Italian poster, WW II, Pearl Harbor

194. REMEMBER PEARL HARBOR, 1942, three-sheet, WW II, Pearl Harbor

195. WAKE ISLAND, 1942, six-sheet, WW II, Pacific

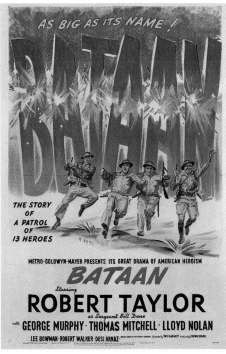

196. BATAAN, 1943, WW II, Pacific

197. BATTLE OF BLOOD ISLAND, 1960, WW II, Pacific

198. OBJECTIVE BURMA, 1945, WW II, Burma

199. FLYING TIGERS, 1942, WW II, Burma

200. YESTERDAY'S ENEMY, 1959, WW II, Burma

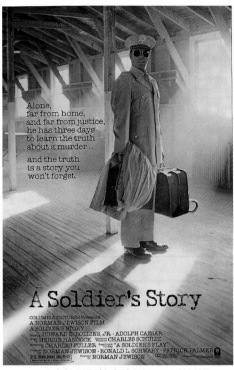

201. A SOLDIER'S STORY, 1984, WW II,
U.S. Home Front

202. SWING SHIFT, 1984, WW II,
U.S. Home Front

203. SWING SHIFT MAISIE, 1943, WW II,
U.S. Home Front

204. THE NEXT OF KIN, 1942, WW II, U.S. Home Front

205. ROSIE THE RIVETER, 1944, WW II, U.S. Home Front

206. SINCE YOU WENT AWAY, 1944, WW II, U.S. Home Front

207. THE CLOCK, 1945, WW II, U.S. Home Front

208. MIRACLE IN THE RAIN, 1956, WW II,
U.S. Home Front

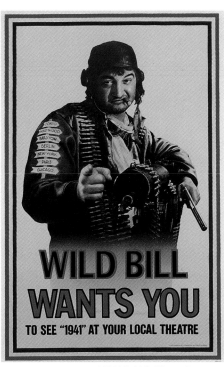

209. 1941, 1979, WW II, U.S. Home Front

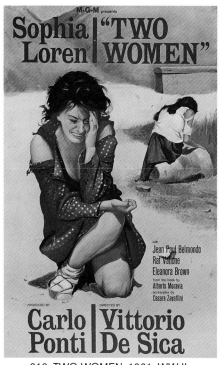

210. TWO WOMEN, 1961, WW II,
Italian Home Front

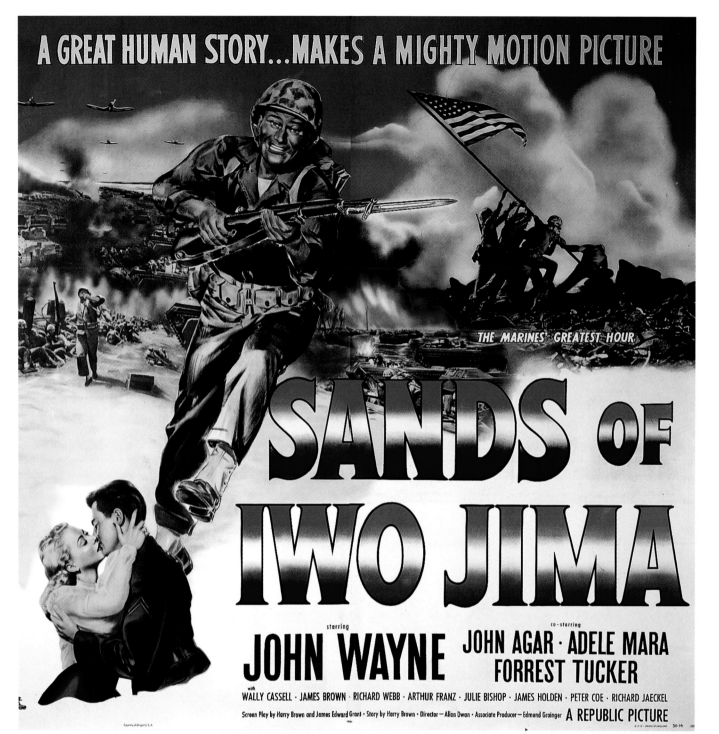

211. SANDS OF IWO JIMA, 1949, six-sheet, WW II, Pacific, U.S.M.C.

212. SANDS OF IWO JIMA, 1949, Italian poster, WW II, Pacific, U.S.M.C.

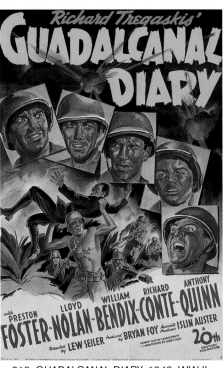

213. GUADALCANAL DIARY, 1943, WW II, Pacific, U.S.M.C.

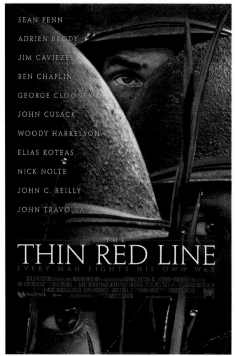

214. THE THIN RED LINE, 1998, WW II, Pacific, U.S.M.C.

215. FLYING LEATHERNECKS, 1951, WW II, Pacific, U.S.M.C.

216. HALLS OF MONTEZUMA, 1951, WW II, Pacific, U.S.M.C.

217. MARINE RAIDERS, 1944, WW II, Pacific, U.S.M.C.

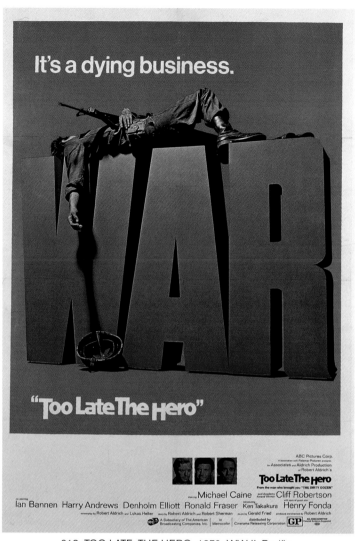

218. TOO LATE, THE HERO, 1970, WW II, Pacific

219. BATTLE CRY, 1955, Italian poster, WW II,
Pacific, U.S.M.C.

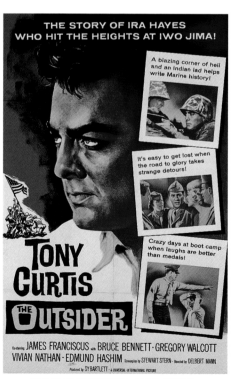

220. THE OUTSIDER, 1962, WW II,
Pacific, U.S.M.C.

221. OKINAWA, 1952, WW II, Pacific, U.S.M.C.

222. THEY WERE EXPENDABLE, 1945, WW II, Pacific, U.S. Navy

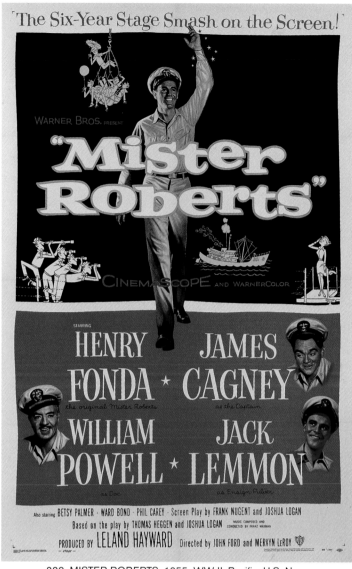

223. MISTER ROBERTS, 1955, WW II, Pacific, U.S. Navy

224. RUN SILENT, RUN DEEP, 1958, WW II,
Pacific, U.S. Navy

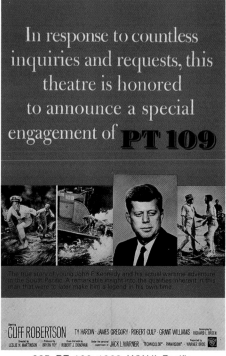

225. P.T. 109, 1963, WW II, Pacific,
U.S. Navy

226. MIDWAY, 1976, WW II, Pacific,
U.S. Navy

227. BOMBARDIER, 1943, WW II, Pacific,
U.S. Army Air Force

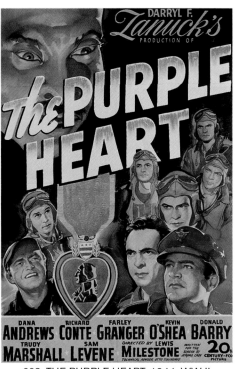

228. THE PURPLE HEART, 1944, WW II,
Pacific, U.S. Army Air Force

229. THE WILD BLUE YONDER, 1952,
WW II, Pacific, U.S. Army Air Force

230. THIRTY SECONDS OVER TOKYO, 1944, WW II, Pacific,
U.S. Army Air Force

231. THE BAMBOO BLONDE, 1946, WW II, Pacific,
U.S. Army Air Force

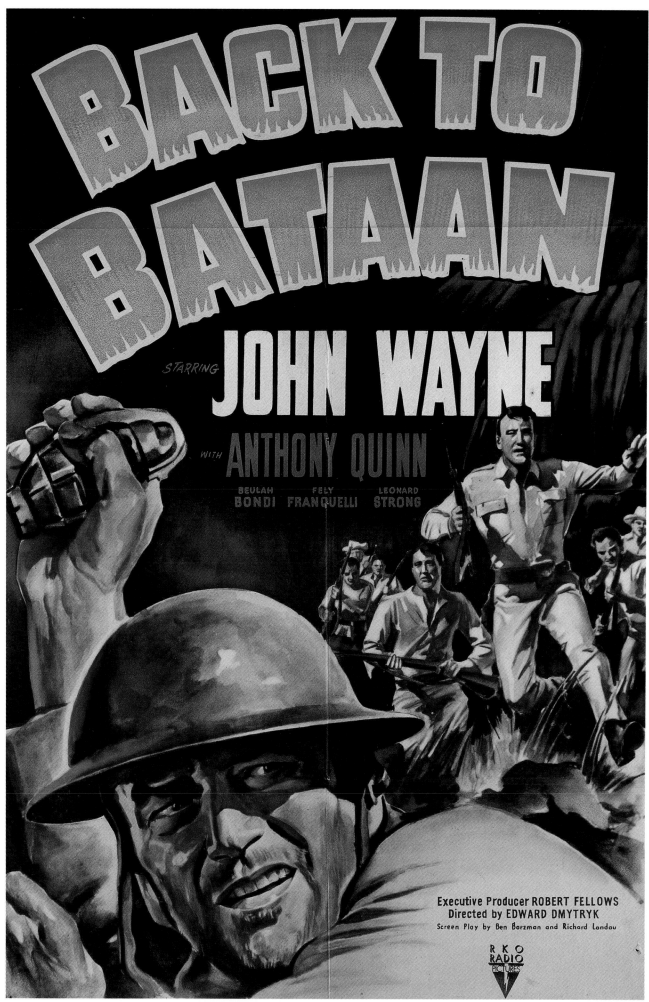

232. BACK TO BATAAN, 1945, WW II, Pacific, U.S. Army

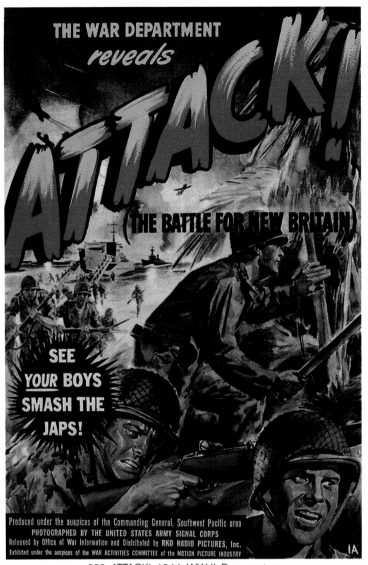

233. ATTACK!, 1944, WW II, Documentary

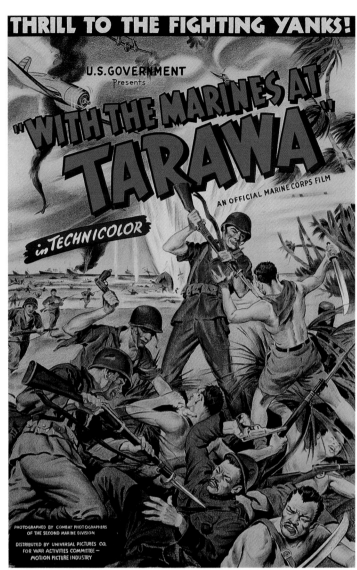

234. WITH THE MARINES AT TARAWA, 1944, WW II, Documentary

235. THE CITY THAT STOPPED HITLER, 1943,
WW II, Documentary

236. MENACE OF THE RISING SUN, 1942,
WW II, Documentary

237. THE FALL OF BERLIN, 1945,
Argentinian poster, WW II, Documentary

238. THE TRUE GLORY, 1945, WW II, Documentary

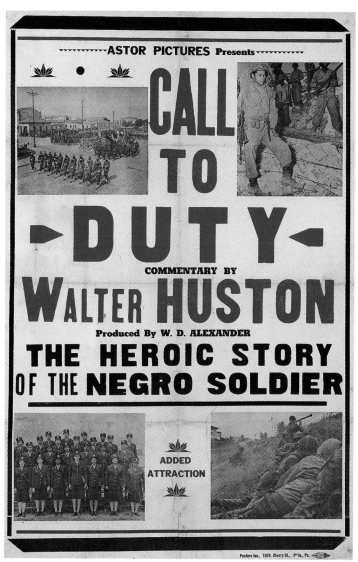

239. CALL TO DUTY, 1945, WW II, Documentary

240. THE FINEST HOURS, 1964, WW II, Documentary

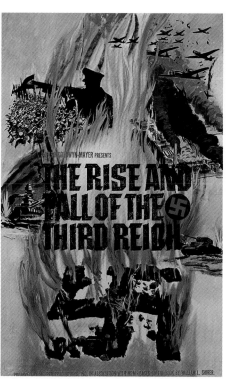

241. THE RISE AND FALL OF THE THIRD REICH, 1967, WW II, Documentary

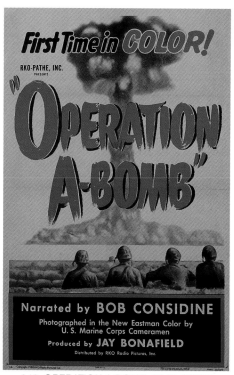

242. OPERATION A-BOMB, 1948, WW II, Documentary

243. THE BEST YEARS OF OUR LIVES, 1946, WW II, Returning Home

244. A BELL FOR ADANO, 1945, WW II, Returning Home

245. THE MEN, 1950, WW II, Returning Home

246. JUDGEMENT AT NUREMBERG, 1961, British quad, WW II, Nazi War Trial

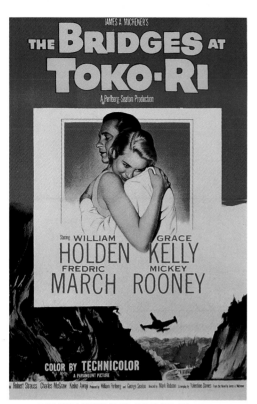

247. THE BRIDGES AT TOKO-RI, 1954,
Korean War

248. BATTLE HYMN, 1957, Korean War

249. TANK BATTALION, 1958, Korean War

250. WAR IS HELL!, 1964, Korean War

251. RETREAT HELL!, 1952, Italian poster, Korean War

252. ALL THE YOUNG MEN, 1960, Italian poster, Korean War

253. BATTLE FLAME, 1959, Korean War

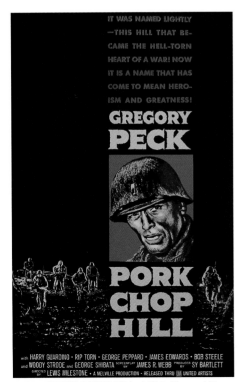

254. PORK CHOP HILL, 1959, Korean War

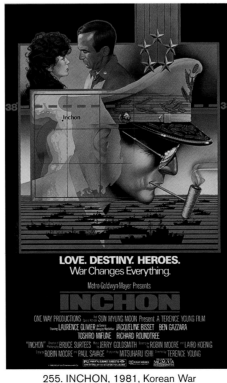

255. INCHON, 1981, Korean War

256. THE IRON CURTAIN, 1948, Cold War

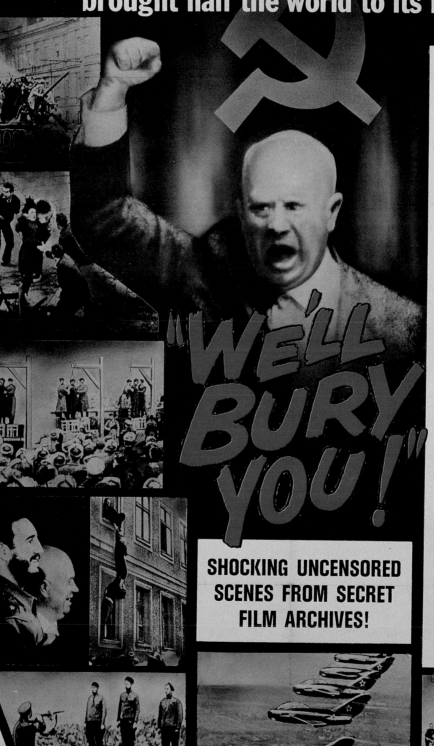

RED...OR DEAD!

The master plan of Communist terror that brought half the world to its knees!

257. WE'LL BURY YOU!, 1962, Cold War, Documentary

258. STRATEGIC AIR COMMAND, 1955, Cold War

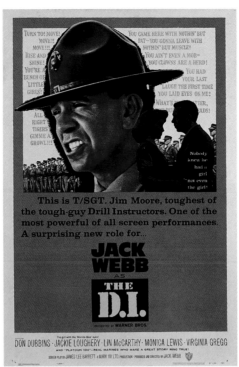

259. THE D.I., 1957, Cold War

260. JET PILOT, 1957, Cold War

261. THE REBEL CASTRO, c.1960, Cold War

262. FAIL SAFE, 1964, Cold War

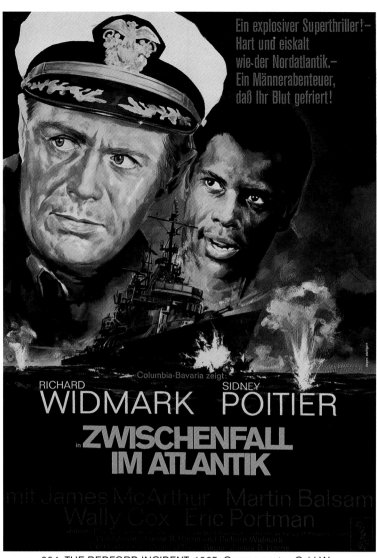

263. DR. STRANGELOVE, 1964, Cold War

264. THE BEDFORD INCIDENT, 1965, German poster, Cold War

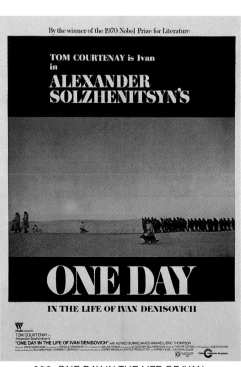

265. ICE STATION ZEBRA, 1968, Cold War

266. ONE DAY IN THE LIFE OF IVAN DENISOVICH, 1971, Cold War

267. THE GREAT SANTINI, 1979, Cold War

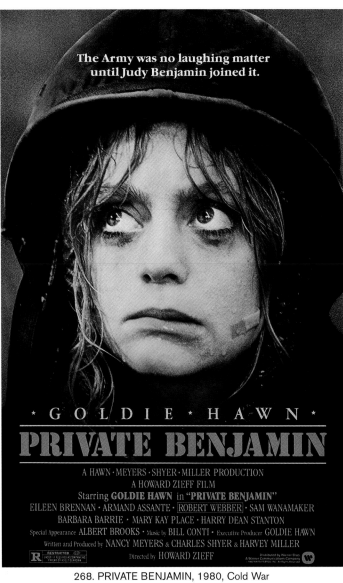

The Army was no laughing matter
until Judy Benjamin joined it.

* GOLDIE * HAWN *

PRIVATE BENJAMIN

268. PRIVATE BENJAMIN, 1980, Cold War

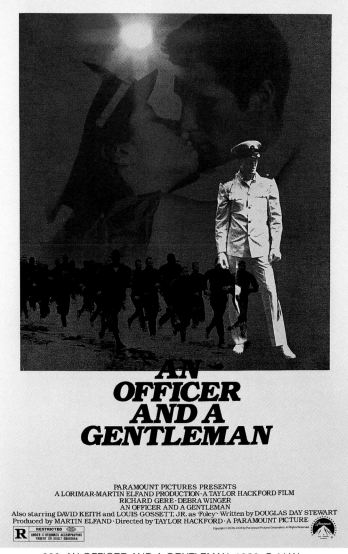

269. AN OFFICER AND A GENTLEMAN, 1982, Cold War

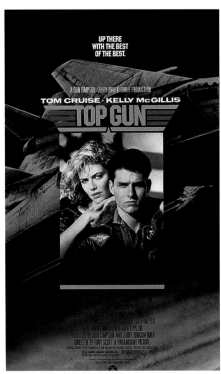

270. TOP GUN, 1986, Cold War

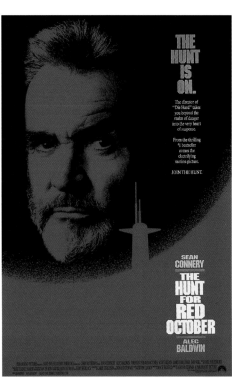

271. THE HUNT FOR RED OCTOBER, 1990,
Cold War

272. G.I. JANE, 1997, Cold War

273. THE GREEN BERETS, 1968, German poster, Vietnam War

274. A YANK IN VIET-NAM, 1964,
Vietnam War

275. GO TELL THE SPARTANS, 1978,
Vietnam War

276. THE BOYS IN COMPANY C, 1977,
Vietnam War

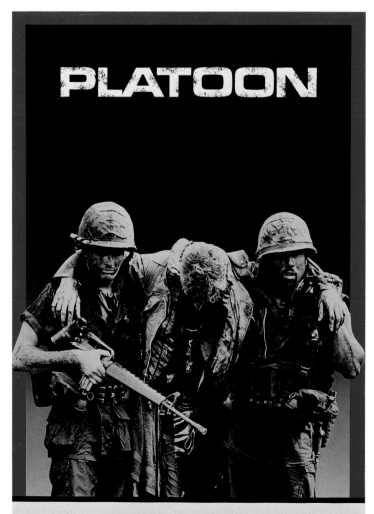

277. PLATOON, 1986, Vietnam War

278. GOOD MORNING VIETNAM, 1987, Vietnam War

279. APOCALYPSE NOW, 1979, Vietnam War

FRANCIS COPPOLA'S FILM "APOCALYPSE NOW"

地獄の黙示録

戦争は魅力的だ。そこには美と魅力があるに違いない。さもなければ人類はこんなにも始終戦争を繰り返しているはずはない。──フランシス・コッポラ

280. APOCALYPSE NOW, 1979, Japanese poster, Vietnam War

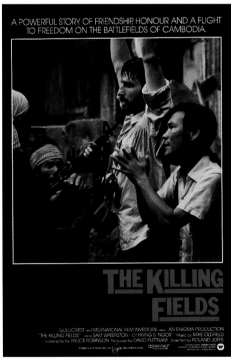

281. THE KILLING FIELDS, 1984, Vietnam War

282. HAMBURGER HILL, 1987, Vietnam War

283. FULL METAL JACKET, 1987, Vietnam War

THE DEER HUNTER

EMI Films present

ROBERT DE NIRO IN A **MICHAEL CIMINO** Film **THE DEER HUNTER**

co-starring

JOHN CAZALE · JOHN SAVAGE · MERYL STREEP · CHRISTOPHER WALKEN

Music composed by STANLEY MYERS · Director of Photography VILMOS ZSIGMOND, A.S.C.
Associate Producers MARION ROSENBERG · JOANN CARELLI · Production Consultant JOANN CARELLI
Story by MICHAEL CIMINO, DERIC WASHBURN and LOUIS GARFINKLE, QUINN K. REDEKER
Screenplay by DERIC WASHBURN · Produced by BARRY SPIKINGS · MICHAEL DEELEY · MICHAEL CIMINO and JOHN PEVERALL

Directed by **MICHAEL CIMINO**

Technicolor® · Panavision® ᗕᗒ DOLBY SYSTEM ® Stereo Distributed by EMI Films Limited ©1978 by EMI Films, Inc.

284. THE DEER HUNTER, 1978, English poster, Vietnam War

285. COMING HOME, 1978, Return from Vietnam War

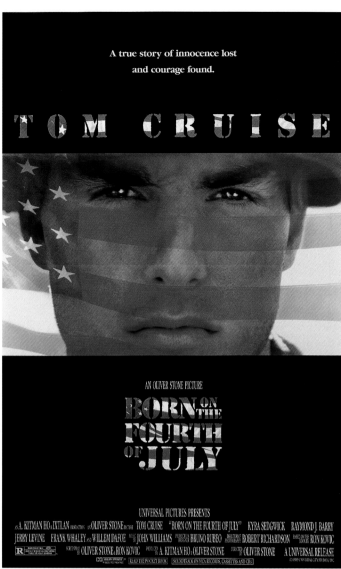

286. BORN ON THE FOURTH OF JULY, 1989, Return from Vietnam War

287. THE DEER HUNTER, 1978, lobby card, Return from Vietnam War

288. CAST A GIANT SHADOW, 1966, Israeli Independence

289. EXODUS, 1960, Italian poster, Israeli Independence

290. BATTLE OF ALGIERS, 1966, Algerian War

291. COMMANDO, 1962, Algerian War

292. SINAI COMMANDOS, 1968, Six Day War

293. THE DOGS OF WAR,
1981, insert, African Rebellion

294. UNDER FIRE, 1983, War in Nicaragua

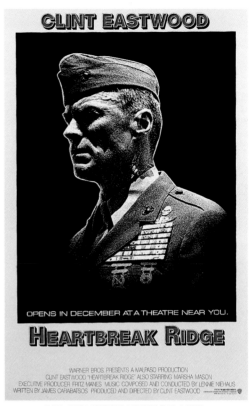

295. HEARTBREAK RIDGE, 1986,
War in Grenada

296. THREE KINGS, 1999, Gulf War

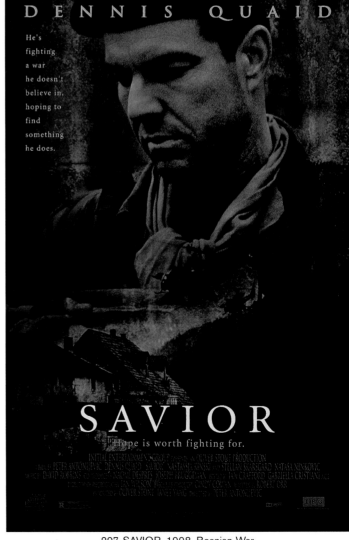

297. SAVIOR, 1998, Bosnian War

WAR MOVIE POSTERS INDEX

WAR MOVIE POSTERS INDEX